THIS BOOK BELONGS TO

....

ENQUIRIES REF

NAME

ADDRESS

EMAIL

TEL

DETAILS

TYPE

BUDGET

ENQUIRIES REF

NAME

ADDRESS

EMAIL

TEL

DETAILS

TYPE

BUDGET

ENQUIRIES REF

NAME

ADDRESS

EMAIL

TEL

DETAILS

TYPE

BUDGET

ENQUIRIES REF

NAME

ADDRESS

EMAIL

TEL

DETAILS

TYPE

BUDGET

ENQUIRIES REF

NAME

ADDRESS

EMAIL

TEL

DETAILS

TYPE

BUDGET

ENQUIRIES | REF |

| NAME |
| ADDRESS |
| EMAIL |

| TEL |
| DETAILS |
| TYPE |

| BUDGET |

ENQUIRIES REF

NAME

ADDRESS

EMAIL

TEL

DETAILS

TYPE

BUDGET

ENQUIRIES REF

NAME

ADDRESS

EMAIL

TEL

DETAILS

TYPE

BUDGET

ENQUIRIES REF

NAME

ADDRESS

EMAIL

TEL

DETAILS

TYPE

BUDGET

ENQUIRIES REF

NAME

ADDRESS

EMAIL

TEL

DETAILS

TYPE

BUDGET

ENQUIRIES REF

NAME

ADDRESS

EMAIL

TEL

DETAILS

TYPE

BUDGET

ENQUIRIES REF

NAME

ADDRESS

EMAIL

TEL

DETAILS

TYPE

BUDGET

ENQUIRIES REF

NAME

ADDRESS

EMAIL

TEL

DETAILS

TYPE

BUDGET

ENQUIRIES REF

NAME

ADDRESS

EMAIL

TEL

DETAILS

TYPE

BUDGET

ENQUIRIES REF

NAME

ADDRESS

EMAIL

TEL

DETAILS

TYPE

BUDGET

ENQUIRIES REF

NAME

ADDRESS

EMAIL

TEL

DETAILS

TYPE

BUDGET

ENQUIRIES REF

NAME

ADDRESS

EMAIL

TEL

DETAILS

TYPE

BUDGET

ENQUIRIES REF

NAME

ADDRESS

EMAIL

TEL

DETAILS

TYPE

BUDGET

ENQUIRIES REF

NAME

ADDRESS

EMAIL

TEL

DETAILS

TYPE

BUDGET

ENQUIRIES REF

NAME

ADDRESS

EMAIL

TEL

DETAILS

TYPE

BUDGET

ENQUIRIES REF

NAME

ADDRESS

EMAIL

TEL

DETAILS

TYPE

BUDGET

ENQUIRIES REF

NAME

ADDRESS

EMAIL

TEL

DETAILS

TYPE

BUDGET

ENQUIRIES REF

NAME

ADDRESS

EMAIL

TEL

DETAILS

TYPE

BUDGET

ENQUIRIES REF

NAME

ADDRESS

EMAIL

TEL

DETAILS

TYPE

BUDGET

ENQUIRIES   REF

NAME

ADDRESS

EMAIL

TEL

DETAILS

TYPE

BUDGET

ENQUIRIES REF

NAME

ADDRESS

EMAIL

TEL

DETAILS

TYPE

BUDGET

ENQUIRIES REF

NAME

ADDRESS

EMAIL

TEL

DETAILS

TYPE

BUDGET

ENQUIRIES   REF

NAME

ADDRESS

EMAIL

TEL

DETAILS

TYPE

BUDGET

ENQUIRIES REF

NAME

ADDRESS

EMAIL

TEL

DETAILS

TYPE

BUDGET

ENQUIRIES | REF

NAME

ADDRESS

EMAIL

TEL

DETAILS

TYPE

BUDGET

ENQUIRIES REF

NAME

ADDRESS

EMAIL

TEL

DETAILS

TYPE

BUDGET

ENQUIRIES REF

NAME

ADDRESS

EMAIL

TEL

DETAILS

TYPE

BUDGET

ENQUIRIES REF

NAME

ADDRESS

EMAIL

TEL

DETAILS

TYPE

BUDGET

ENQUIRIES REF

NAME

ADDRESS

EMAIL

TEL

DETAILS

TYPE

BUDGET

ENQUIRIES REF

NAME

ADDRESS

EMAIL

TEL

DETAILS

TYPE

BUDGET

ENQUIRIES REF

NAME

ADDRESS

EMAIL

TEL

DETAILS

TYPE

BUDGET

ENQUIRIES REF

NAME

ADDRESS

EMAIL

TEL

DETAILS

TYPE

BUDGET

ENQUIRIES REF

NAME

ADDRESS

EMAIL

TEL

DETAILS

TYPE

BUDGET

ENQUIRIES REF

NAME

ADDRESS

EMAIL

TEL

DETAILS

TYPE

BUDGET

ENQUIRIES REF

NAME

ADDRESS

EMAIL

TEL

DETAILS

TYPE

BUDGET

ENQUIRIES REF

NAME

ADDRESS

EMAIL

TEL

DETAILS

TYPE

BUDGET

ENQUIRIES REF

NAME

ADDRESS

EMAIL

TEL

DETAILS

TYPE

BUDGET

ENQUIRIES REF

NAME

ADDRESS

EMAIL

TEL

DETAILS

TYPE

BUDGET

ENQUIRIES REF

NAME

ADDRESS

EMAIL

TEL

DETAILS

TYPE

BUDGET

ENQUIRIES REF

NAME

ADDRESS

EMAIL

TEL

DETAILS

TYPE

BUDGET

ENQUIRIES REF

NAME

ADDRESS

EMAIL

TEL

DETAILS

TYPE

BUDGET

ENQUIRIES REF

NAME

ADDRESS

EMAIL

TEL

DETAILS

TYPE

BUDGET

ENQUIRIES REF

NAME

ADDRESS

EMAIL

TEL

DETAILS

TYPE

BUDGET

ENQUIRIES REF

NAME

ADDRESS

EMAIL

TEL

DETAILS

TYPE

BUDGET

ENQUIRIES REF

NAME

ADDRESS

EMAIL

TEL

DETAILS

TYPE

BUDGET

ENQUIRIES

REF

NAME

ADDRESS

EMAIL

TEL

DETAILS

TYPE

BUDGET

ENQUIRIES REF

NAME

ADDRESS

EMAIL

TEL

DETAILS

TYPE

BUDGET

ENQUIRIES | REF

NAME

ADDRESS

EMAIL

TEL

DETAILS

TYPE

BUDGET

ENQUIRIES REF

NAME

ADDRESS

EMAIL

TEL

DETAILS

TYPE

BUDGET

ENQUIRIES | REF

NAME

ADDRESS

EMAIL

TEL

DETAILS

TYPE

BUDGET

ENQUIRIES REF

NAME

ADDRESS

EMAIL

TEL

DETAILS

TYPE

BUDGET

ENQUIRIES | REF

NAME

ADDRESS

EMAIL

TEL

DETAILS

TYPE

BUDGET

ENQUIRIES REF

NAME

ADDRESS

EMAIL

TEL

DETAILS

TYPE

BUDGET

ENQUIRIES REF

NAME

ADDRESS

EMAIL

TEL

DETAILS

TYPE

BUDGET

ENQUIRIES REF

NAME

ADDRESS

EMAIL

TEL

DETAILS

TYPE

BUDGET

ENQUIRIES REF

NAME

ADDRESS

EMAIL

TEL

DETAILS

TYPE

BUDGET

ENQUIRIES REF

NAME

ADDRESS

EMAIL

TEL

DETAILS

TYPE

BUDGET

ENQUIRIES REF

NAME

ADDRESS

EMAIL

TEL

DETAILS

TYPE

BUDGET

ENQUIRIES REF

NAME

ADDRESS

EMAIL

TEL

DETAILS

TYPE

BUDGET

ENQUIRIES REF

NAME

ADDRESS

EMAIL

TEL

DETAILS

TYPE

BUDGET

ENQUIRIES REF

NAME

ADDRESS

EMAIL

TEL

DETAILS

TYPE

BUDGET

ENQUIRIES REF

NAME

ADDRESS

EMAIL

TEL

DETAILS

TYPE

BUDGET

ENQUIRIES REF

NAME

ADDRESS

EMAIL

TEL

DETAILS

TYPE

BUDGET

ENQUIRIES REF

NAME

ADDRESS

EMAIL

TEL

DETAILS

TYPE

BUDGET

ENQUIRIES | REF

NAME

ADDRESS

EMAIL

TEL

DETAILS

TYPE

BUDGET

ENQUIRIES REF

NAME

ADDRESS

EMAIL

TEL

DETAILS

TYPE

BUDGET

ENQUIRIES REF

NAME

ADDRESS

EMAIL

TEL

DETAILS

TYPE

BUDGET

ENQUIRIES REF

NAME

ADDRESS

EMAIL

TEL

DETAILS

TYPE

BUDGET

ENQUIRIES REF

NAME

ADDRESS

EMAIL

TEL

DETAILS

TYPE

BUDGET

ENQUIRIES REF

NAME

ADDRESS

EMAIL

TEL

DETAILS

TYPE

BUDGET

ENQUIRIES REF

NAME

ADDRESS

EMAIL

TEL

DETAILS

TYPE

BUDGET

ENQUIRIES REF

NAME

ADDRESS

EMAIL

TEL

DETAILS

TYPE

BUDGET

ENQUIRIES REF

NAME

ADDRESS

EMAIL

TEL

DETAILS

TYPE

BUDGET

ENQUIRIES REF

NAME

ADDRESS

EMAIL

TEL

DETAILS

TYPE

BUDGET

ENQUIRIES REF

NAME

ADDRESS

EMAIL

TEL

DETAILS

TYPE

BUDGET

ENQUIRIES REF

NAME

ADDRESS

EMAIL

TEL

DETAILS

TYPE

BUDGET

ENQUIRIES REF

NAME

ADDRESS

EMAIL

TEL

DETAILS

TYPE

BUDGET

ENQUIRIES REF

NAME

ADDRESS

EMAIL

TEL

DETAILS

TYPE

BUDGET

ENQUIRIES REF

NAME

ADDRESS

EMAIL

TEL

DETAILS

TYPE

BUDGET

ENQUIRIES REF

NAME

ADDRESS

EMAIL

TEL

DETAILS

TYPE

BUDGET

ENQUIRIES REF

NAME

ADDRESS

EMAIL

TEL

DETAILS

TYPE

BUDGET

ENQUIRIES REF

NAME

ADDRESS

EMAIL

TEL

DETAILS

TYPE

BUDGET

ENQUIRIES REF

NAME

ADDRESS

EMAIL

TEL

DETAILS

TYPE

BUDGET

ENQUIRIES REF

NAME

ADDRESS

EMAIL

TEL

DETAILS

TYPE

BUDGET

ENQUIRIES REF

NAME

ADDRESS

EMAIL

TEL

DETAILS

TYPE

BUDGET

ENQUIRIES REF

NAME

ADDRESS

EMAIL

TEL

DETAILS

TYPE

BUDGET

ENQUIRIES REF

NAME

ADDRESS

EMAIL

TEL

DETAILS

TYPE

BUDGET

ENQUIRIES | REF

NAME

ADDRESS

EMAIL

TEL

DETAILS

TYPE

BUDGET

ENQUIRIES REF

NAME

ADDRESS

EMAIL

TEL

DETAILS

TYPE

BUDGET

ENQUIRIES   REF

NAME

ADDRESS

EMAIL

TEL

DETAILS

TYPE

BUDGET

ENQUIRIES REF

NAME

ADDRESS

EMAIL

TEL

DETAILS

TYPE

BUDGET

ENQUIRIES | REF

NAME

ADDRESS

EMAIL

TEL

DETAILS

TYPE

BUDGET

ENQUIRIES REF

NAME

ADDRESS

EMAIL

TEL

DETAILS

TYPE

BUDGET

ENQUIRIES REF

NAME

ADDRESS

EMAIL

TEL

DETAILS

TYPE

BUDGET

ENQUIRIES REF

NAME

ADDRESS

EMAIL

TEL

DETAILS

TYPE

BUDGET

ENQUIRIES REF

NAME

ADDRESS

EMAIL

TEL

DETAILS

TYPE

BUDGET

ENQUIRIES REF

NAME

ADDRESS

EMAIL

TEL

DETAILS

TYPE

BUDGET

ENQUIRIES REF

NAME

ADDRESS

EMAIL

TEL

DETAILS

TYPE

BUDGET

ENQUIRIES REF

NAME

ADDRESS

EMAIL

TEL

DETAILS

TYPE

BUDGET

ENQUIRIES REF

NAME

ADDRESS

EMAIL

TEL

DETAILS

TYPE

BUDGET

ENQUIRIES REF

NAME

ADDRESS

EMAIL

TEL

DETAILS

TYPE

BUDGET

ENQUIRIES REF

NAME

ADDRESS

EMAIL

TEL

DETAILS

TYPE

BUDGET

ENQUIRIES REF

NAME

ADDRESS

EMAIL

TEL

DETAILS

TYPE

BUDGET

ENQUIRIES REF

NAME

ADDRESS

EMAIL

TEL

DETAILS

TYPE

BUDGET

ENQUIRIES REF

NAME

ADDRESS

EMAIL

TEL

DETAILS

TYPE

BUDGET

ENQUIRIES REF

NAME

ADDRESS

EMAIL

TEL

DETAILS

TYPE

BUDGET

ENQUIRIES REF

NAME

ADDRESS

EMAIL

TEL

DETAILS

TYPE

BUDGET

ENQUIRIES REF

NAME

ADDRESS

EMAIL

TEL

DETAILS

TYPE

BUDGET

ENQUIRIES REF

NAME

ADDRESS

EMAIL

TEL

DETAILS

TYPE

BUDGET

ENQUIRIES REF

NAME

ADDRESS

EMAIL

TEL

DETAILS

TYPE

BUDGET

ENQUIRIES REF

NAME

ADDRESS

EMAIL

TEL

DETAILS

TYPE

BUDGET

ENQUIRIES REF

NAME

ADDRESS

EMAIL

TEL

DETAILS

TYPE

BUDGET

ENQUIRIES REF

NAME

ADDRESS

EMAIL

TEL

DETAILS

TYPE

BUDGET

ENQUIRIES REF

NAME

ADDRESS

EMAIL

TEL

DETAILS

TYPE

BUDGET

ENQUIRIES

REF

NAME
ADDRESS
EMAIL

TEL
DETAILS
TYPE

BUDGET

www.ingramcontent.com/pod-product-compliance
Lightning Source LLC
Chambersburg PA
CBHW060421220526

45465CB00008B/2966